PROJECTS ABOUT
Ancient Rome

Karen Frankel

Marshall Cavendish
Benchmark

New York

Acknowledgments

For their help and participation in the activities, I would like to thank:
David Carstensen, Paula Cangialosi, Dalton Fields, Jacob Frankel, Amelia Jadow, Benjamin Jadow, Gabrielle Morelli, Jake Regensberg, and Sawyer Stettin.

Benchmark Books
Marshall Cavendish
99 White Plains Road
Tarrytown, NY 10591-9001
www.marshallcavendish.us

Text Copyright © 2006 by Marshall Cavendish Corporation
Illustrations and Map Copyright ©2006 by Marshall Cavendish Corporation

Library of Congress Cataloging-in-Publication Data
Frankel, Karen.
Projects about ancient Rome/by Karen Frankel.
p. cm.—(Hands-on history)
Summary: "Includes social studies projects taken from the ancient Romans"—Provided by publisher.
Includes bibliographical references and index.
ISBN-13: 978-0-7614-2260-0
ISBN-10: 0-7614-2260-9
1. Rome—Civilization—Study and teaching (Elementary)—Activity programs—Juvenile literature. 2. Rome—Social life and customs—Study and teaching (Elementary)—Activity programs—Juvenile literature. I. Title. II. Series.
DG77.F72 2006
937—dc22
2006002815

Title page: Severus Arch in the *Forum Romanum*, Rome, Italy
Maps by XNR Productions
Illustrations by Rodica Prato
Photo research by Joan Meisel

Alamy: 10, 27, *Mary Evans Picture Library*; *Art Resource, NY*: 18, *SEF*; 19, Werner Forman; 22, *Scala*; 43, Erich Lessing; *Corbis*: 1, G. Rossenbach/*Zefa/Corbis;* 4, B. Kohlhas/Zefa; 31, John & Lisa Merrill; 34, Richard Glover; *North Wind Picture Archives*: 6, 11, 24

Printed in China

1 3 5 6 4 2

Contents

᪐

The *Forum Romanum*, or Roman Forum, was the economic, political, and religious center of ancient Rome.

1

Introduction

You experience the heritage of ancient Rome every day—from the words you use to the milestones you see along the highway that tell you how far you've gone. For a thousand years Rome was the center of Western Civilization, influencing the way of life for people from Britain to most of Europe, North Africa and Egypt, and parts of the Middle East. Buildings and structures from ancient Rome still stand today. We speak languages with Latin roots, and many of our ideas about laws and government are based on ancient Rome.

This book will help you understand how the ancient Romans lived. You'll see how the people dressed and make your own **tunics**. You'll count using the same Roman numerals they did, and learn the Latin alphabet. You'll discover why Romans were considered master builders as you construct an arch and make a **milestone**. You'll design a **mosaic**, make a **laurel wreath**, and form an **amphora**. And you'll cook two authentic Roman dishes. As you do these activities you'll learn even more about the ways the ancient Romans did things.

After winning one battle, the famous Roman general Julius Caesar wrote, "Veni, vidi, vici," which translates to, "I came, I saw, I conquered." May you do the same as you learn about ancient Rome.

A Vast Empire

The Roman Empire began as a single city, Rome, on the banks of the Tiber River. By 272 BCE (see page 8) Rome controlled all of Italy.

The Roman Empire kept expanding, first by conquering its neighbors and then fighting wars with other nations that were nearby. Some of the best-known battles occurred during the **Punic Wars** with Rome's enemy the Carthaginians.

Carthage, a powerful city-state in North Africa, controlled parts of Spain as well as various islands in the Mediterranean. During the Second Punic War (218 BCE–201 BCE), Hannibal, a Carthaginian general, led an army of forty thousand men and thirty-seven elephants into Italy. He defeated the Romans in many bitter battles, but he was not able to win the war.

By the second century CE (see page 8) the Roman Empire was at its greatest, stretching from Britain to Asia. There were Roman **provinces** throughout most of the known world. As the Roman Empire grew, it spread its way of life.

Hannibal returns victorious to Carthage, seated on his last surviving elephant.

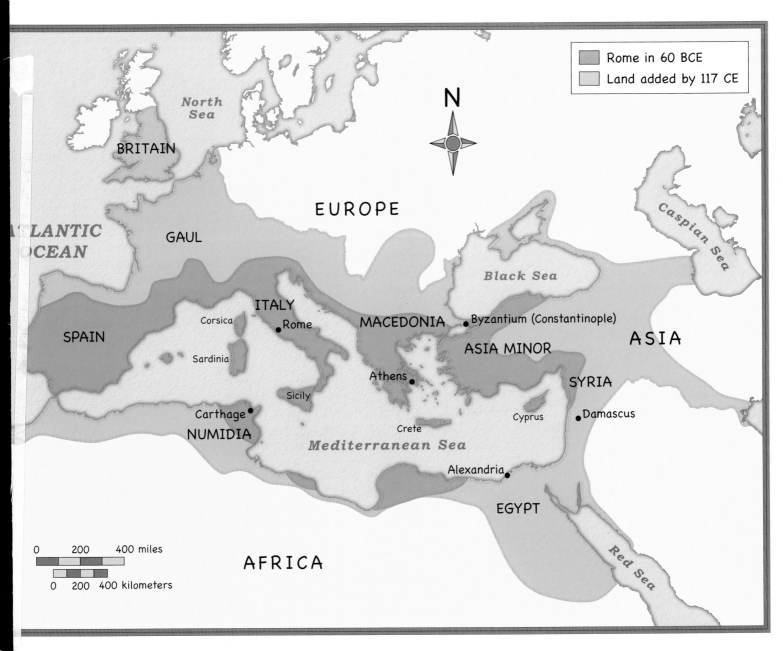

At the height of its power, the Roman Empire spread across three continents: Africa, Asia, and Europe.
This map shows how the empire expanded from the years 60 BCE (dark green) to 117 CE (light green).

The Calendar and BCE

The Romans began dating their years from the founding of Rome. When the Christian calendar was introduced in the sixth century, it started with the year 1. Years prior to year 1 had BC after them. BC means "before Christ." Because many people are not Christians, BC was changed to BCE, which means "before the Common Era." Dates with BCE after them go backward. For example, 200 BCE is longer ago than 100 BCE.

When the calendar was invented, it used Roman numerals, which did not include zero. So there is no year zero. The year 1 BCE is followed by the year 1 CE.

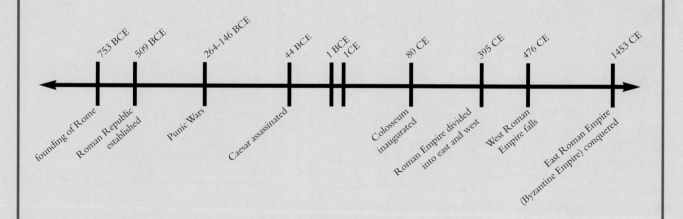

2

Early Rome

According to legend, Rome was founded by Romulus in 753 BCE. There are often different versions of a legend. In one version Romulus and his twin brother, Remus, were abandoned and left for dead. But they were found by a wolf, who fed them with her milk and kept them alive. When the twins grew up, they decided to build a city near the place where they had been abandoned. Rome is a city of seven hills, and Remus and Romulus fought over the exact hill where Rome should be founded. Remus was killed when he jumped over the walls around Romulus's choice, the Palatine Hill. Romulus became the first king of Rome.

For almost two hundred and fifty years, longer than the United States has been a nation, the Romans were ruled by kings, with the aid of the Senate. Senators came from the richest families in Rome. These families were known as **patricians**. Other Roman citizens were known as **plebeians**. They were working-class people, not as rich as the patricians. Many other people living in Rome were slaves, people who had been captured during wars and their children.

In 509 BCE, Rome became a republic in which the power resided with the Roman Senate and two consuls. Consuls were senators who were elected to run the city. The consuls usually held office for one year. The Roman Republic lasted until the time of Caesar.

Patrician women wore tunics made of costly silk, linen, or wool.

Tunic

It was the day of Lucius's coming-of-age ceremony. "I can finally get a grown-up toga," he said to his younger sister, Julia.

"I know," said Julia. "Your new toga is all white. It won't have the purple hem that your old one has. I went with mother to the **fuller**'s to get the cloth." A fuller washed new wool and laundered dirty garments. "It really smelled." Fullers used urine along with other ingredients to wash the cloth.

"It's so big," said Julia, looking at the vast expanse of material.

"Of course," said Lucius. "It needs to be three times as tall as I am in order to drape properly. But I can't wait to wear it."

In ancient Rome only boys and men who were Roman citizens could wear togas. But everyone—men and women, boys and girls, citizens and slaves—wore tunics. Men wore them underneath their togas, while women would wear them as their everyday garment.

Boys up to the age of sixteen wore togas with a purple border. The Emperor's toga was all purple. Someone in mourning wore a black, blue, or gray toga.

You will need:

- material
- tape measure
- scissors

- yarn or string
- pen or chalk that can write on material

1. Measure your shoulders and add 2 inches to determine the width of the material.

2. Measure the distance between your shoulders and knees, or ankles, and double it to determine the length. Boys' togas were usually knee length, while girls' togas could reach their ankles.

3. Cut the material in a long rectangle, and fold the material lengthwise.

4. Make a dot in the center of the fold.

5. Measure 3 inches from the dot and mark it.

6. Measure 4 inches from the dot in either direction along the fold and mark the spots.

7. Draw a semicircle connecting the dots.

8. Cut out the semicircle. You will be cutting through two layers of cloth.

9. Take a short piece of yarn or string and tie the material between the neck hole and the side. Do the same thing on the other side.

10. Put the tunic on over your head.

11. Take a long length of yarn and make a belt.

Bread

"I'm hungry," said Rosa. "Is there anything to eat?"

"Here," said Rosa's mother, handing her some coins. "Run down to the baker and get some bread."

Rosa ran down the three flights of stairs from their apartment in the center of the city. She went through the crowded streets to the baker. He was up before dawn making loaves of bread and rolls. Many Roman families did not have kitchens and were only able to cook over little fires. They bought much of the food they ate from food shops and street vendors.

The baker knew Rosa because she came almost every day. "Do you want one or two loaves?" he asked.

"Just one," answered Rosa.

"Here," he said, handing her the loaf. Then with a smile, he gave her a little bun that had cheese on the top. "This is just for you."

You will need:

- 1 package active dry yeast
- 1 ½ cups warm water
- 3 ¾ to 4 cups all-purpose flour
- 1 teaspoon honey
- 1 teaspoon salt
- 1 tablespoon olive oil
- nonstick spray
- fork or spoon for mixing
- mixing bowls—one large and one small
- cookie sheet
- dish towel
- empty food cans with straight edges, muffin tin, pastry cloth (optional)

1. Wash your hands, and ask an adult to help.

2. Mix the yeast with ½ cup warm water and 1 teaspoon honey in the small mixing bowl. (The Romans did not have sugar, and used honey for sweetening.) The mixture will foam and double in size in a few minutes.

3. Measure 3 ¾ cups flour into the large bowl.

4. Add the salt.

5. Add 1 cup warm water, and mix with a fork or spoon.

6. Add the yeast mixture to the flour, and mix until the flour and water form a ball. You may need to add a little more water or flour.

7. Put the dough on a surface covered with a little flour. You can use a pastry cloth or floured countertop.

8. Knead the dough for 4 to 8 minutes, adding flour to keep the dough from sticking to your hands. To knead, press the heels of your hands into the dough, pushing it away. Then fold the dough and push it again (see illustrations). When you can press your fingers into the dough and the dough springs back, you've done enough kneading. Let the dough rest for a few minutes.

1.

9. Wash and dry the large mixing bowl, and put 1 tablespoon of olive oil in it, swirling it around to cover the inside of the bowl.

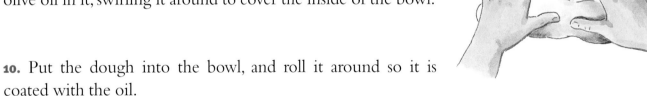

10. Put the dough into the bowl, and roll it around so it is coated with the oil.

2.

11. Put a dish towel on top, and place the bowl in a warm spot. You can take pieces of the dough and put them into a can or a muffin tin that you've oiled or greased. Only fill them up halfway, and cover with a dish towel.

12. The dough will double in size in about an hour. If you've used a muffin tin or can, it will be easy to tell because the dough will be above the top rim.

13. Preheat the oven to 400°F.

14. Grease or spray the bottom of a cookie sheet, and place the round ball of dough on it. Pat it down. If you have dough in cans, place them on the cookie sheet too.

15. Bake at 400°F for 35 to 40 minutes, until the top is golden brown.

16. Test the doneness by tapping the loaf. If it sounds hollow, it's done. If you don't hear a hollow sound, let it bake for another 5 minutes.

17. Take it out and let it cool.

Milestone

"The Romans build the best roads in the world," said Titus's father as they rode along the **Appian Way**. "See how smooth the surface is. And when it rains, the water just runs down the side."

"Why do we have such good roads?" asked Titus.

"It's because of the army. Having a good, straight road makes it easier for our troops to move quickly. Look," he said, pointing to the side of the road. "Do you know what that is?"

Titus saw a big pillar. It said, "Rome V."

"It's a milestone. We only have five miles to go to get to Rome."

Romans used milestones to measure distance. Milestones told how far a spot on the road was from the center of the city. They measured distance in Roman miles. A Roman mile was about one thousand paces, or 4,860 feet. Is it longer or shorter than our miles?

This Roman milestone was erected in 218 CE.

The Appian Way is the oldest and most famous road built by the ancient Romans. It is more than 350 miles (560 kilometers) long and went from Rome to Brindisi, the port for ships to Greece.

You will need:

- a container to mold your milestone Use a paper cup that is waxed on the inside, an empty box from a bar of hand soap, or a small yogurt container.
- plaster of Paris
- water
- disposable mixing bowl
- Popsicle or other disposable mixing stick
- petroleum jelly
- pencil or ballpoint pen

1. Use your fingers to grease inside a cup or soap box or yogurt container with petroleum jelly. Mix plaster of Paris and water—two parts plaster, one part water.

2. Pour the mixture into the container. Let it set for approximately 20 minutes. It needs to be hard but still soft enough that you can inscribe on it.

3. Tear off the paper cup or box.

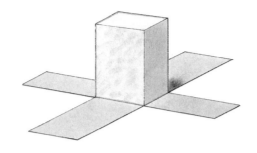

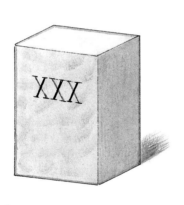

4. Using a pencil or ballpoint pen, write the number of miles in Roman numerals you are from the capital of your state. (See page 37 for Roman numerals.)

Gaius Julius Caesar (100-44 BCE), military genius and leader of the Roman world.

3

The Age of Caesar

Julius Caesar may be the best-known Roman of all. A brilliant general, Caesar led the Roman troops to victories in Spain. Back in Rome, he was elected consul and with two other Romans formed the First **Triumvirate**, a group of three people who tried to influence Roman politics. Caesar then went to Gaul (modern-day France) to serve as governor. While there, he began a ten-year campaign to bring the area under Roman rule. He also made a brief expedition into Britain, which was the first step in the Roman invasion of the island.

The Roman Senate ordered Caesar to give up his command because he was becoming too powerful and successful. Caesar decided to fight the Senate's action. He made a fateful decision to lead his army back to Rome, crossing the Rubicon River, the border between Gaul and Italy, on his way. Today, "to cross the Rubicon" means taking an action that you can't turn back from.

Caesar and his army took Italy with little problem. He then went to Egypt, where he installed Cleopatra as queen, and went on to further victories in Africa and Spain.

Caesar declared himself dictator for life, taking away much of the power of the Senate. This action was also the beginning of the end of the Roman Republic. On March 15—the Ides of March—44 BCE, Caesar was assassinated.

Julius Caesar wrote several books describing his conquests. He changed the calendar and named a month—July—after himself. And he's the subject of the play *Julius Caesar*, by the great playwright William Shakespeare.

In 44 BCE, Julius Caesar was assassinated in the Roman Senate. Two years after his death, the Senate declared him a god.

English to Latin

"Marcus, what did you do in school today?" asked his mother.

"We learned the alphabet," he answered.

"Very good. Can you recite it?"

"A, B, C, D, E, F, G, H, I, K, L, M, N, O, P, Q, R, S, T, V, X, Y, Z—all twenty-three letters. And I learned how to write my name." Marcus wrote on his clay tablet: MARCVS.

The English alphabet has twenty-six letters; the Latin alphabet, twenty-three. What English letters are not in the Latin alphabet? (See the bottom of the page for the answer.)

(Answer: J, U, W—In classical Latin, I and J were interchangeable, as were U and V. Julius Caesar's name would be spelled IVLIVS CAESAR.)

Some languages are known as Romance languages. These languages—which include French, Spanish, Italian, Portuguese, and Romanian—are based on Latin. Other languages, such as English, have many words that come from the Latin.

Match the English word to the Latin word that means the same thing. Here's a hint. Try matching the first letter. Write your answers on a separate sheet of paper. (The answers are at the bottom of the page.)

ENGLISH WORD	LATIN WORD
a. mother	1. antique
b. second	2. actor
c. ancient	3. difficilis
d. actor	4. expello
e. many	5. familia
f. difficult	6. hora
g. peace	7. mater
h. hour	8. multi
i. rose	9. pax
j. time	10. poeta
k. king	11. populas
l. drive out	12. rosa
m. people	13. rex
n. family	14. secundus
o. villa, country house	15. tempus
p. poet	16. villa

Laurel Wreath

"Hurry," said Gaius to his friend Titus. "We don't want to miss seeing the parade." Whenever the Romans achieved a great victory, they held a **triumph**, which included a big parade. The two boys ran to get a good viewing spot to watch the procession of senators, musicians, prisoners of war, and white bulls and oxen for sacrifices. They were followed by the general, riding in a chariot with his family, and his troops.

"I see him," said Titus. "He's standing up in that chariot. And he's holding a laurel branch and wearing a crown of laurel."

"That's because laurel is a symbol of victory," said Gaius. "When we achieve great victories, we'll be able to wear laurel wreaths, too."

A Roman general, on the right, wears a laurel wreath. Many Roman emperors wore the laurel wreath as a sign of their power and success.

27

1. Measure the circumference of your head and add 2 inches.

2. Cut strips of construction paper approximately $1/2$ inch wide.
You need enough strips to go around your head with a little overlap. Glue the strips together end to end to make 1 long strip.

3. Trace the laurel leaf provided in the illustration, and cut it out to make a pattern, or use a real leaf. Make your laurel leaves about 5 inches long and 2 inches wide.

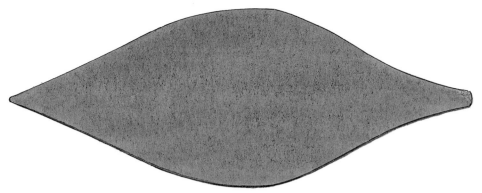

4. Cut out nine to fifteen leaves. You can cut several at one time by folding your paper in half or thirds.

5. Paste your laurel leaves on the thin strip, overlapping them in the same pattern as seen in the illustration. Leave the last few inches of the strip without any leaves.

6. Measure the wreath against your head. Hold your finger where the two ends overlap.

7. Glue the overlapping ends together.

Mosaic

Marius and Livia watched as workmen came to their villa. They were carrying bags and bags of **tesserae**, little tiles that they would use to make a mosaic.

"I wonder how many tesserae they'll need to do the floor in the entryway?" asked Livia.

"Probably thousands," said Marius. "Each one is so tiny that it will take a lot to cover the area."

"Do you know what pattern Mother decided on?" asked Livia. Marius shook his head. "No, but I hope she picked a picture instead of a design. I like them better."

Romans used mosaics as floor coverings and to make pictures of people and things they liked. Some mosaics were black and white, while others had many different colors in them. The mosaic tiles, or tesserae, could be made of clay, stone, pottery, glass, or bricks.

Mosaics in wealthy homes were often statements to visitors about the owner's place in society.

1. Draw a picture of your mosaic on your background paper. You might want to draw a fish or a snake, a portrait of a friend, or a geometric pattern.

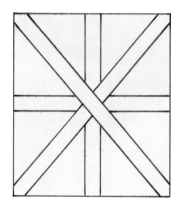

2. Cut out little squares of different colored paper—1 inch by 1 inch is a good size.

3. Paste the squares on your drawing, following your outline. If you want, you can make a background out of different colored squares.

4. Paste a border around your mosaic using squares of just one color.

The Colosseum is one of the finest examples of Roman architecture and engineering. Many modern arenas and stadiums incorporate important features from the Colosseum such as the oval shape, the tiers of seating, and the underground staging area.

4

The Roman Empire

After the assassination of Caesar three leaders formed the Second Triumvirate. These leaders were Octavius, who was Caesar's teenage grandnephew and heir; Mark Antony, who was Caesar's friend; and Lepidus, who had been Caesar's second-in-command. They killed Caesar's assassins, and then fought among themselves to gain control of the government. Octavius won, defeating Antony, who had gone to Egypt and married Cleopatra. Both Antony and Cleopatra committed suicide. Egypt became a Roman province and the empire grew even larger.

Octavius was the first ruler of the Roman Empire. He called himself Augustus, and August, the eighth month of our calendar, is named after him.

For the next two hundred years the Roman Empire reached its greatest heights of power and prosperity, expanding north to Britain and east to the Persian Gulf. This period was called the Pax Romana, or Roman Peace.

The Roman Empire had more than seventy emperors following Augustus. Some ruled well, others badly.

In 395 CE the Roman Empire was divided into east and west. The West Roman Empire became weaker as Vandals, Visigoths, and other groups invaded the country. The West Roman Empire fell in 476 CE. The East Roman Empire, which had its capital in Constantinople, survived for another nine hundred years.

The Colosseum

In 80 CE there was huge excitement in Rome. It was the opening day of the Colosseum, an **amphitheater** where **gladiators** would fight each other and wild animals, and trained animals would perform tricks for the crowd. Workers had been building the Colosseum for eight years, and they would continue to build for another few years before it was complete.

"Will you see all the animals?" asked Janus.

"Yes," said his father, nodding his head. They had visited the zoo outside Rome where the animals were kept.

"Where will you be sitting?"

"I'll be sitting in the tenth row." He showed Janus his ivory token or **tessera**, which served as a ticket to get in. It had the number of the entrance, the seat, and the row carved on it. Although admission was free, everyone needed a ticket to get in.

"I wish I could go," said Janus.

"When you're older," said his father. The spectacles at the Colosseum were too bloody for children. Even women were only permitted to sit far away from the activities, in the highest seats.

Roman Numerals

The Colosseum had eighty entrances. Two were for the emperor and two were for the gladiators. The other seventy-six entrances were for the public, and each one of these entrances was numbered with Roman numerals.

Roman numerals are equal to the following numbers:

I	1
V	5
X	10
L	50
C	100
D	500
M	1000

When a Roman numeral is to the left of another Roman numeral of greater value, you subtract the value. For example, IV = 4 (5 minus 1 = 4). If the numeral is to the right, you add the value. For example, VIII = 8 (5 plus 3 = 8).

What entrance would you go in if your ticket read:

I
III
XXII
VIII
LX
XL
LVII
XIX or XVIIII
IL
XIII

Arch

The Romans were master builders. They invented concrete, which made it possible to build structures that would last for many generations. To build the Colosseum, they used stone arches for the outer walls. Stone arches are much stronger than walls made of solid stone. And a building made completely out of solid stone would have collapsed under its own weight.

Roman arches are still standing in places across Europe and are used for decoration in many parks. Are there any Roman arches in your city?

You will need:

- bar of oval soap (such as Dove or Pears) and its box
- paper towels
- clay
- dish of water
- dull knife to cut clay

---

1. Open the soap box carefully and take out the soap. Fold up two paper towels and put them in the bottom of the box. Put the soap back in the box on top of the paper towels.

2. Cut or mold two pieces of clay the same height and width and depth as the soap box, approximately 4 inches by 1 inch by 1 $\frac{1}{2}$ inches. You can measure them against the box. Make sure they can stand up by themselves.

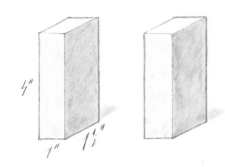

3. Make the arch bricks.
You'll need seven bricks that are 1 $\frac{1}{2}$ inches deep by 1 inch wide and slightly wider at the top (1 inch) than at the bottom ($\frac{3}{4}$ of an inch).

4. Place the large pieces of clay against the sides of the soap box. Stack the small bricks, one at a time, on the large pieces of clay, following the shape of the soap. Put the narrowest part of the brick next to the soap. Make sure the bricks are stuck to each other. Build up from either side. Put the center brick in last. This is called the keystone.

5. Now take the soap and soap box away. Does your arch stay up by itself?

Amphora

Livia and her father watched as slaves unloaded the cargo from one of the big ships that had just come in from Greece.

"I bet that amphora is full of olive oil," said Livia, pointing to the big jar being carried by one of the slaves.

"Look at how easy it is for them to carry it," said her father. The slave was holding the amphora by one of the side handles and the knob on the bottom.

"But how do they keep the **amphorae** standing upright?"

"They don't need to on the ship," said her father. "The boat can hold more of them if they're placed on their sides. But when it's necessary, they just make a little hole in the floor so each amphora can stand upright."

You will need:

- clay
- stick for smoothing the clay
- water

---

1. Take a small ball of clay and make it into a thin flat patty about the size of your palm.

2. Make thin rolls of clay, and use them to build up the sides of the amphora by forming the rolls into rings, placing the first ring on the patty (base), and placing additional rings on top of each other.

3. Make the amphora wider in the middle by using longer lengths of clay. Make it narrower as you get to the top by using shorter lengths of the clay rolls. At the very top, it should be able to be closed with a cork.

4. Smooth the clay with your fingers and water, or with a stick and water.

5. Make two handles and attach them with clay. Then, make a knob and attach it to the bottom.

Dates

Claudius wandered down to the kitchen to get a treat. But the cook, a slave named Fabius, and all his helpers ignored him. "Why is everyone in such a rush?" he asked.

"Your parents are having guests for dinner tonight. We have to get ready," answered Fabius. "I've been preparing for days."

He waved his hand. "Look."

There were nine stuffed **dormice**, ready to go into the oven. Lettuce and cut leeks were nearby. A whole fish was being boned and scaled. One slave was arranging a wooden hen on top of pastry eggs. And another slave was putting grapes and apples and pears on a big platter.

"I still have a lot to do," he said. He saw Claudius looking at the dates greedily. "Here, you can have one before I stuff them. Or do you want to wait, help me crush the nuts for filling, and then have one when they're cooled?"

Dates stuffed with nuts and cooked in honey were Claudius's favorite treat. What do you think he said?

This mosaic shows a slave carrying a plate at a banquet. Wealthy Romans held banquets frequently, and served everything from roasted peacock to pastries.

You will need:

- ten dates with the pits removed
- nuts—walnuts and/or pignolas (pine nuts). You will need five or six pine nuts for each date and 2 tablespoons crushed walnuts for ten dates.
- $1/2$ cup honey
- small saucepan or frying pan
- hammer or mallet or stone

1. Wash your hands, and ask an adult to help.

2. Put the walnuts in a plastic bag, and then crush them, using a hammer or mallet or stone.

3. Stuff each date with five or six pine nuts, or the crushed walnuts.

4. Put the stuffed dates in a small saucepan or frying pan.

5. Add $1/2$ cup honey.

6. Bring to a boil.

7. Simmer for 5 to 7 minutes, stirring occasionally, until the outer layer of the date's skin starts coming off. It's very thin and like an onion skin.

8. Take the pan off the stove, pour the mixture into a container, and let it cool completely.

Glossary

amphitheater: An oval or round structure with seats around a center open area.

amphora, amphorae (plural): A jar used to carry wine and oil. Amphorae usually had two handles on the sides and a knob or handle on the bottom.

Appian Way: A Roman highway built in 312 BCE, going from Rome to Brindisi, 350 miles away.

dormouse, dormice (plural): A small mouse, or rodent, that looks like a squirrel.

fuller: The person who washes and cleans cloth. The fuller was the Roman version of today's dry cleaner.

gladiators: People who fought against each other or wild animals in the Colosseum or other arena.

laurel wreath: A crown made from leaves of the laurel tree.

legend: A story passed down from earlier times. It may or may not be true.

milestone: A marker measuring the number of miles from a certain point.

mosaic: A picture or pattern made up of little pieces or cubes of tile, pottery, glass or other material called **tesserae.**

patricians: Rich Roman families.

plebeians: Working-class Romans.

provinces: Land conquered by Rome and governed by a Roman official.

Punic Wars: Three wars between Rome and Carthage which lasted on and off from 264 BCE to 146 BCE.

tessera, tesserae (plural): Small pieces of tile, pottery, glass or other materials. They were used to make mosaics. Tesserae made of ivory were used as tickets for the Colosseum.

triumph: Honors given to a victorious general which included a parade.

Triumvirate: A group of three men governing a city or nation.

tunic: The short-sleeved or sleeveless garment worn by ancient Romans and Greeks.

Metric Conversion Chart

You can use the chart below to convert from U. S. measurements to the metric system.

Weight
1 ounce = 28 grams
½ pound (8 ounces) = 227 grams
1 pound = .45 kilogram
2.2 pounds = 1 kilogram

Liquid volume
1 teaspoon = 5 milliliters
1 tablespoon = 15 milliliters
1 fluid ounce = 30 milliliters
1 cup = 240 milliliters (.24 liter)
1 pint = 480 milliliters (.48 liter)
1 quart = .95 liter

Length
¼ inch = .6 centimeter
½ inch = 1.25 centimeters
1 inch = 2.5 centimeters

Temperature
100°F = 40°C
110°F = 45°C
350°F = 180°C
375°F = 190°C
400°F = 200°C
425°F = 220°C
450°F = 235°C

About the Author

Karen Frankel has written award-winning media for children of all ages. She lives in New York City.

Find Out More

Books

Connolly, Peter, text by Andrew Solway. *Ancient Rome.* New York: Oxford
University Press, 2001.

Corbishley, Mike. *What Do We Know About The Romans?* New York: Peter Bedrick
Books, 1991.

James, John, and Louise James. *How We Know About The Romans.* Chicago: Peter Bedrick
Books, 1997.

James, Simon. *Ancient Rome, Eyewitness Books.* New York: Dorling Kindersley Book, 1990.

Macdonald, Fiona, and Mark Bergin. *The Roman Colosseum.* Inside Story Series. Chicago:
Peter Bedrick Books, 1998.

Sheehan, Sean. *Ancient Rome.* History Beneath Your Feet Series. Austin, Texas: Raintree
Steck-Vaugh Company, 2000.

Whittock, Martyn. *The Roman Empire.* New York: Peter Bedrick Books, 1991, 1993.

Web Sites

Ancient Rome
www.crystalinks.com/rome.html

BBC's Home Page for Roman History
www.bbc.co.uk/schools/romans/

Daily Life in Ancient Rome
members.aol.com/Donnclass/Romelife.html

The Roman Empire—Children's Section
www.roman-empire.net/childrens/

Index